S E A S O N A L
POTS AND PLANTERS

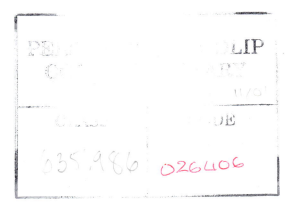

SEASONAL
POTS AND PLANTERS

EVERYTHING YOU NEED TO KNOW TO CREATE SHOW-STOPPING PLANTINGS FOR ALL SEASONS

Stephanie Donaldson

southwater

This edition is published by Southwater

Southwater is an imprint of
Anness Publishing Limited
Hermes House
88-89 Blackfriars Road
London SE1 8HA
tel. 020 7401 2077
fax 020 7633 9499

Distributed in the UK by
The Manning Partnership
251-253 London Road East
Batheaston
Bath BA1 7RL
tel. 01225 852 727
fax 01225 852 852

Distributed in the USA by
Anness Publishing Inc.
27 West 20th Street
Suite 504
New York NY 10011
fax 212 807 6813

Distributed in Australia by
Sandstone Publishing
Unit 1, 360 Norton Street
Leichhardt
New South Wales 2040
tel. 02 9560 7888
fax 02 9560 7488

1 3 5 7 9 10 8 6 4 2

Publisher *Joanna Lorenz*
Managing Editor *Judith Simons*
Project Editor *Mariano Kälfors*
Designer *Janet James*
Photography *Marie O'Hara*
Production Controller *Don Campaniello*

Previously published as part of a larger compendium, *The Ultimate Container Gardener.*

ACKNOWLEDGEMENTS
All projects were created by Stephanie
Donaldson and photographed by
Marie O'Hara unless otherwise stated.

CONTRIBUTORS
Clare Bradley: p 32. Blaise Cooke: pp
22, 23, 70, 71, 83. Tessa Evelegh: pp
10t, 13, 16.

PHOTOGRAPHERS
Peter Anderson: pp 7tr, 96. John
Freeman: pp 2–4, 6, 7br, 10m, 12,
16m, 16b, 17b, 18r, 19mr, 22–24, 27r,
30–35, 37–41, 46, 67–72, 74, 75, 78,
79, 83–90, 92, 93, 95. Don Last: p
29r. Debbie Patterson: pp 1, 10t, 13,
16m, 16b, 17b, 18l. Peter McHoy: pp
11, 28, 29l.

Contents

Introduction

Pots and planters are a wonderful way to celebrate each season. Enjoy the arrival of spring with cheerful bulbs, create an instant summer with bright annuals and biennials, and use evergreen and woody perennials to provide autumnal colour and foliage in the winter.

ABOVE: *These brilliant tulips in full flower herald the end of winter and the beginning of spring.*

The right container for the right setting adds a special touch. Watering cans make a novel and eye-catching focal point and colour-fully painted pots can evoke hot and lazy days in the Mediterranean. Arranging individual pots of flowering plants within a container and replacing a single pot when it is over will maintain a vibrant display for longer.

Be creative with seasonal colours and enhance your garden all through the year.

ABOVE: *A summer wall basket of yellow-leaved helichrysum and blue felicia emphasize the soft yellow flowers of marguerite.*

OPPOSITE: *Formally clipped box topiaries are ideal for a classic setting given plenty of room.*

RIGHT: *Grouping these other-wise ordinary containers creates a focal point and takes advantage of spare space.*

Getting Started

To enjoy your container garden from its inception, begin by choosing the plantings according to the colour scheme you desire, then choose containers that will show off the plants to their full advantage. Plants suitable for containers can be grown as part of a hanging garden or in baskets or half-pots filled with the right compost (soil mix) fixed to a wall, or in standing pots. Then, with regular feeding and watering and keeping a watchful eye open for signs of pests and diseases, you are certain to have a success on your hands.

Providing year-round colour

Containers are traditionally used for creating extra, lavish colourful effects in summer. With a little thought and careful planning you can enjoy delightful containers all year round.

First Signs of Spring

Early spring bulbs burst into life as soon as winter loosens its grip. Even on chilly, rainy days, pots planted with small bulbs – snowdrops, crocuses, scillas and *Iris reticulata* – will provide splashes of clear colour on the patio or window-sills, and can be briefly brought indoors, if you like, for an early taste of spring. Primulas and polyanthus look great in containers, too. If you grow lily-of-the-valley in the garden, pot up a few roots and bring them inside: they'll come into bloom weeks early.

ABOVE AND LEFT: *Plants might not flourish in the garden border all year round, but you can still have some delightful plants every day of the year. Here, small pots of lily-of-the-valley, dwarf irises, crocuses and primroses brighten up a warm day in early spring.*

Summer Blooms

Summer is, of course, the highlight of the container gardener's year, giving the opportunity for lovely creative plantings. Deciding which plants to use is an enjoyable task.

RIGHT: *For a really eye-catching container, be different. A large potted mix, featuring summer bedding plants topped by a lanky white fuchsia, is encircled by a rustic woven sheep feeder. The effect is heightened by tufts of grass packed into the gaps.*

FAR RIGHT: *A flamboyant show of billowing annuals.*

Autumn Highlights

Grow one or two autumn-glory shrubs in tubs that you can bring out when you need a final burst of colour on the patio.

Ceratostigma willmottiamum has compact growth and lovely autumn foliage tints while still producing blue flowers. Berries can also be used as a feature, and you can usually buy compact gaultherias already bearing berries in your garden centre.

ABOVE: *Potted chrysanthemums (here flanked by ericas) are an easy and excellent way of prolonging bright summer colours into autumn.*

Winter Colour

Some winter-flowering shrubs can be used in tubs, such as *Viburnum tinus* and *Mahonia* x *media* 'Charity'. Try being bold with short-term pot plants such as Cape heathers (*Erica hyemalis* and *E. gracilis*) and winter cherries (*Solanum capsicastrum* and similar species and hybrids). You will have to throw them away afterwards, but they will look respectable for a few weeks even in cold and frosty winter weather.

HOW TO PROTECT PLANTS FROM FROST

Many of the most dramatic summer patio shrubs – like daturas and oleanders – must be taken into a frost-free place for the winter. Others that are frost-tolerant but of borderline hardiness in cold areas, like the bay (*Laurus nobilis*), or that are vulnerable to frost and wind damage to the leaves (such as *Choisya ternata* 'Sundance') need a degree of winter protection. It is a pity to lose these magnificent patio plants for the sake of a little forethought as autumn draws to a close. Shrubs that are fairly tough and need little protection from the worst weather can be covered with horticultural fleece, or bubbly plastic. If you use fleece, you may be able to buy it as a sleeve (ideal for winter protection for shrubs in tubs).

1 Insert four or five canes around the edge of the pot. Cut the plastic to size. Allow for an overlap over the pot.

2 Wrap it around the plant, allowing a generous overlap. For particularly vulnerable plants, use more than one layer. Securely tie the protection around the pot. For very delicate plants, bring the material well down over the pot, to keep the root-ball warm. Leave the top open for ventilation and to permit watering if necessary.

GARDENER'S TIP

If covering with fleece, tie the top together (moisture will be able to penetrate, and tying the top will help to conserve warmth).

OPPOSITE: *Smooth, topiarized box balls and pyramids catch the eye at any time of year. You can buy them ready styled or, better still, raise your own cuttings and shape them as you wish.*

Types of container

One of the challenges of container gardening is finding the right container for the right setting. You can now quite readily buy a whole range of lovely containers, for example, waist-high, Italian olive oil jars make a terrific focal point – big and bold and stylish. At the other end of the scale, you can be as imaginative as you like. You could use a Wellington boot or an old shoe for an engaging, quirky touch. In between, of course, the choice is huge: rustic terracotta, voguish metal or brightly painted cans, Mediterranean style.

It is important to consider the final setting when you are buying a container. A rustic tub may look charming under the window of a thatched cottage, but inappropriate outside a formal town house. Bear proportions in mind and, for example, choose a windowbox that exactly fits the sill. It is also worth noting that the weight of a container, when filled with compost (soil mix) and freshly watered, will be considerably greater than when empty. Think twice before packing your roof terrace or balcony with heavy pots: the structure may not be able to cope. And never leave a container on a window-sill from where it could fall down into the street.

Stone troughs

NOT SO READILY AVAILABLE BUT DEFINITELY WORTH LOOKING AT.

Advantages – durable and attractive.

Disadvantages – very heavy and expensive.

Pots and barrels

VERSATILE AND PRACTICAL.

Advantages – maintenance-free and versatile.

Disadvantages – heavy to move.

Wooden windowboxes

GIVE A WOODEN CONTAINER AN ORIGINAL LOOK WITH YOUR OWN COLOUR SCHEME.

Advantages – you can change the look to suit any new planting scheme.

Disadvantages – the boxes require occasional maintenance.

Terracotta windowboxes

AVAILABLE IN A WIDE RANGE OF SIZES AND STYLES.

Advantages – look good and appear even better with age.

Disadvantages – heavy, and may be damaged by frost.

Galvanized tin

TIN HAS MOVED FROM THE UTILITARIAN TO THE FASHIONABLE.

Advantages – an interesting variation from the usual materials.

Disadvantages – drainage holes required.

Lightweight fibre windowboxes

PLAIN AND PRACTICAL.

Advantages – look rustic, and have a rich brown colour.

Disadvantages – short life-span.

Baskets

CAN BE USED AS WINDOWBOXES PROVIDED THEY ARE GENEROUSLY LINED WITH MOSS BEFORE PLANTING.

Advantages – lightweight and attractive.

Disadvantages – plant pots must be removed for watering, or the base of the basket will be soaked and rot.

Types of hanging baskets

Before you choose the plants and plan how to arrange them, decide first what style of hanging basket you are going to display them in. Garden centres stock a huge variety, which are all easy to work with and hang. Hanging baskets are made from plastic-coated wire, wrought-iron and galvanized wire.

Hanging baskets

VARIED AND PRACTICAL.

Advantages – look lovely planted.

Disadvantages – need to be lined before use.

Novelty containers

HUGELY UNDERRATED. USE ANYTHING FROM WATERING-CANS OR TYRES TO SHOES.

Advantages – witty and fun.

Disadvantages – possible short life-span.

The best plants for containers

Annuals and Biennials

Whether you raise them yourself from seed in the greenhouse or on the kitchen window-sill, or buy them in strips from the garden centre for an instant effect, fast-growing annuals and biennials will quickly and cheaply fill baskets and boxes and flower prolifically all summer to produce eye-catching effects. Choose compact varieties that will not need support. Trailing annuals such as lobelia, nasturtiums and dwarf sweet peas are all invaluable for hanging baskets. Some perennial species, including petunias, pelargoniums and busy Lizzies (impatiens), are normally grown as annuals.

Tender Perennials

Beautiful tender and half-hardy plants such as osteospermums, verbenas, pelargoniums, petunias and fuchsias are ideal for containers, where their showy flowers can be fully appreciated. Raise new plants from cuttings for next season. If you buy young, tender plants from the garden centre in the spring, don't be tempted to put newly planted boxes or baskets outside until all danger of frost is past.

ABOVE: *Trailing nasturtiums make a glorious display, providing colour from early summer.*

LEFT: *Petunias and pelargoniums are tender perennials, which are often grown as annuals.*

BELOW: *Containers of spring bulbs such as these yellow tulips cannot fail to delight.*

Evergreen Perennials

Evergreen non-woody perennials such as ajugas, bergenias and *Carex oshimensis* 'Evergold' are always useful for providing colour and foliage in the winter, but look best as part of a mixed planting.

For single plantings, try *Agapanthus africanus* or *A. orientalis* with their blue flowers on tall stems. For a more architectural shape, consider one of the many different eryngiums (sea holly). *E. agavifolium* is particularly attractive, and has greenish-white flowers in late summer.

Border Perennials

Few people bother to grow perennials in containers, but if you have a paved garden, or would like to introduce them to the patio, don't be afraid to experiment. Dicentras, agapanthus, and many ornamental grasses are among the plants that you might want to try, but there are very many more that you should be able to succeed with – and they will cost you nothing if you divide a plant already in the border.

Bulbs

Bulbs, particularly the spring varieties make ideal container plants. Bulbs should be planted at twice the depth of their own length. They can be packed in as tight as you like, and even in layers, so that you get a repeat-showing after the first display. Note that when planting lilies (the white, scented, fail-safe *Lilium regale* is a fine choice if you have never tried them before), they need excellent drainage, so put in an extra layer of grit at the bottom. And to prevent spearing the bulb later on with a plant support, insert this in the compost at the same time.

Shrubs for Tubs

Camellias are perfect shrubs for tubs, combining attractive, glossy evergreen foliage with beautiful spring flowers. *Camellia* x *williamsii* and C. *japonica* hybrids are a good choice. Many rhododendrons and azaleas are also a practical proposition, and if you have a chalky (alkaline) soil this is the best way to grow these plants – provided you fill the container with an ericaceous compost (soil mix).

Many hebes make good container plants (but not for very cold or exposed areas), and there are many attractively variegated varieties. The yellow-leaved *Choisya ternata* 'Sundance' and variegated yuccas such as *Yucca filamentosa* 'Variegata' and *Y. gloriosa* 'Variegata' are also striking shrubs for containers.

For some winter interest, try *Viburnum tinus*.

Topiary for Pots

Topiarized box is ideal for a pot. However, it is relatively slow growing at about 30cm (12in) a year. It may be best to buy a mature, ready-shaped plant, although you miss the fun of doing the pruning.

ABOVE: *If your garden cannot support lime-hating rhododendrons, do not despair. They can easily be grown in pots, in ericaceous compost (soil mix), and will give a wonderful display of colour.*

LEFT: *Pots on plinths and fruit trees in tubs create a marvellous architectural effect, with plenty of striking verticals.*

Trees for Tubs

Trees are unlikely candidates for containers, particularly for small gardens. Fortunately, the restricted root-run usually keeps them compact and they never reach the proportions of trees planted in the ground. Even in a small garden, some height is useful.

Choose trees that are naturally small if possible. Laburnums, crab apples (and some of the upright-growing and compact eating apples on dwarfing rootstocks), *Prunus* 'Amanogawa' (a flowering cherry with narrow, upright growth), and even trees as potentially large as *Acer platanoides* 'Drummondii' (a variegated maple) will be happy in a large pot or tub for a number of years. Small weeping trees also look good. Try *Salix caprea pendula* or *Cotoneaster* 'Hybridus Pendulus' (which has cascades of red berries in autumn). Even the pretty dome-shaped, grey-leaved *Pyrus salicifolia* 'Pendula' is a possibility.

These must have a heavy pot with a minimum inside diameter of 38cm (15in), and a loam-based compost (soil mix). Even then they are liable to blow over in very strong winds unless you pack some other hefty pots around them during stormy weather.

Planting pots and planters

Planting up a container of any size could not be easier, as long as you follow a few basic rules. First, terracotta pots need a layer of material at the bottom to help the water drain away quickly. Plastic pots usually have sufficient drainage holes. Second, always plant into the appropriate size pot; that is, slightly larger than the root-ball. Putting a small plant into a large pot is counter productive. The plant will put on good root growth at the expense of flowers and foliage. Since the hungry root system will drink up water rapidly in summer, check regularly that the soil is not too dry.

ABOVE: *Beautiful, elegant urns do not always need the finest flowering plants. As these twin pots show, even a modest planting works well. Indeed, it is often preferable because it does not detract from the gorgeous containers.*

Maintaining Plants

Large plants can grow in surprisingly small containers. They will not grow to the same height as if they were given a free root run, but should be impressive nonetheless. If possible, remove the top layer of soil every year, and replace it with fresh compost (soil mix). There comes a time, however, when most plants finally outgrow their containers. What then? You can replace the mature plant with a cutting and start again. Alternatively, stick instead to plants that are slow-growing, or which will not rapidly fill their pots with roots. Or root prune.

Root pruning is a remarkably easy technique, which involves removing the plant from the pot in spring, when it is beginning to put on good growth. Either slice away the exterior of the root-ball quite boldly, or snip at it with secateurs. Then replace in the existing pot, filling the gap with fresh compost.

Overwintering

Remember that while tender plants may just survive winter outside in your area, with their roots protected deep below ground, those in pots are much less likely to survive. The roots will be just the thickness of the pot away from encircling snow or icy winds. Bring these plants indoors or, if there's no room, take cuttings before the end of the season.

Planting in Terracotta

Terracotta containers are always popular, but need some preparation before planting.

1 With terracotta it is essential to provide some form of drainage material in the base of the container. When planting in large pots or boxes, recycle broken-up polystyrene (plastic foam) plant trays as drainage material. Lumps of polystyrene are excellent for this use and as they retain warmth they are of additional benefit to the plant.

2 In smaller pots the drainage material can be broken pieces of pot, known as crocks, or gravel.

Planting in Plastic

When buying plastic pots or boxes, check that the drainage holes are open. Some manufacturers mark the holes but leave it to the purchaser to punch or drill them out as required.

Plant Supports

Climbing plants in containers will need support. This can be provided by one or more canes which are pushed into the pot, a free-standing plant frame or a trellis fastened to a wall behind the container.

Planting in Wicker Baskets

If you wish to use a more unconventional container as a windowbox you may need to seal it with a sheet of plastic to prevent leakage.

1 Line the basket with a generous layer of moss which will prevent the compost (soil mix) leaking away.

2 Fill the basket with compost (soil mix), and mix in plant food granules or any organic alternative.

Saucers and Feet

Saucers are available for plastic and clay pots. They act as water reservoirs for the plants, and are used under houseplants to protect the surface they are standing on. Clay saucers must be fully glazed if they are used indoors or they will leave marks. Clay feet are available for terracotta pots. They will prevent the pot becoming waterlogged, but this also means that in a sunny position the pot will dry out very quickly and may need extra watering.

Plastic plant saucers can be used to line and protect containers which are not waterproof, such as this wooden apple-basket.

Planting hanging baskets

When you want colour high up or relating closely to the building, the easiest way is to create a hanging garden, either in baskets or in wall-mounted containers. A purpose-made hanging basket is designed so that as the flowers grow, they cascade through the side and spill over the edge in a joyous show of colour, covering the whole basket. An alternative is to make the basket or container part of the display. Ordinary shopping baskets, buckets, agricultural containers, even kitchen equipment such as colanders, pots and pans, can be used.

Planting and Positioning Hanging Baskets

One hanging basket, alone on a wall, can look rather insignificant. Far better to plant up baskets in pairs, either with similar plants to create an echoing effect, or with clashing, contrasting colours. For a really stunning effect, entirely cover a wall with baskets, but remember that they are very demanding, and will need prolific watering in a dry mid-summer.

If the container is large and in danger of getting too heavy for its support, one trick is to put a layer of broken-up expanded polystyrene (plastic foam), from plant trays or electrical goods packaging, in the bottom of the container. This is lighter than the equivalent amount of compost (soil mix) and provides good drainage. Containers should have drainage holes, and baskets will need lining to stop the soil from being washed out while

you are watering. Liners can be home-made from pieces of plastic sheet cut to size, with a layer of moss tucked between the basket and plastic for a more decorative look. Alternatively, you can use a proprietary liner, made from paper pulp, to fit purpose-made hanging baskets, or coconut matting – which comes in a variety of shapes and sizes to adapt to all kinds of baskets.

Whichever type of container you choose, it needs to be filled with a good compost, and adding fertilizer granules and water-retaining gel can also help promote lush results and make care and maintenance a little easier.

RIGHT: *Hanging baskets filled with pansies create a lovely focal point of gentle colour.*

Preparing Hanging Baskets

The key to successful hanging baskets is in the preparation. Time taken in preparing the basket for planting will be rewarded with a long-lasting colourful display. Slow-release plant food granules incorporated into the compost (soil mix) when planting ensure that the plants receive adequate nutrients throughout the growing season. It is essential to water hanging baskets every day, even in overcast weather, as they dry out very quickly. There are various ways to line a hanging basket.

Choosing a Lining

1 When buying a hanging basket, make sure that the chains are detachable. By unhooking one of the chains, they can be placed to one side of the basket, allowing you to work freely. Either rest the basket on a flat surface, or sit it on a flowerpot.

2 Traditionally, hanging baskets are lined with sphagnum moss. This looks very attractive and plants can be introduced at any point in the side of the basket. As sphagnum moss tends to dry out rather faster than other liners, it is advisable to use a compost (soil mix) containing water-retaining gel with this lining.

3 Coir fibre liners are a practical substitute for moss. Although not as good to look at, the coir will soon be hidden as the plants grow. The slits in the liner allow for planting in the side of the basket.

4 Cardboard liners are clean and easy to use. They are made in various sizes to fit most hanging baskets.

5 Press out the marked circles on the cardboard liner if you wish to plant into the side of the basket.

Underplanting a Hanging Basket

Underplanting helps to achieve a really lush-looking basket and soon conceals the shape of the container under flowers and foliage.

1 Line the lower half of the basket with a generous layer of moss.

2 Rest the root-ball on the moss and gently guide the foliage through the side of the basket.

3 Add more moss to the basket, tucking it carefully around the plants to ensure that they are firmly in place. Add a further row of plants near the top edge of the basket, if required, and continue to line the basket with moss, finishing off with a collar of moss overlapping the rim of the basket. Fill with compost (soil mix).

Propagating plants

Most containers and plants are available from garden centres but raising your own plants from seed or cuttings is far easier than you may think and can be very rewarding. Buying young plants from mail order catalogues is an increasingly popular way of starting a collection.

Seed Sowing

One of the cheapest ways of getting a mass planting is by growing plants from seed. It is fun, can be easy (when growing marigolds, for instance), and you don't need a high-tech greenhouse. Furthermore, if you get hooked on the plants, you can collect your own ripe seed in the autumn for a spring sowing the following year.

Cuttings

If you want to increase your stock of the plants you are already growing in the garden, you can get quick results by taking spring cuttings.

When the cuttings have rooted – this will be immediately obvious because they suddenly perk up – wait for the roots to fill the pot, and then transfer to individual pots.

1 Fill the seed tray with seed compost (soil mix). Gently firm and level the surface by pressing down on the compost using a tray of the same size. When sowing large seeds, such as sunflowers or marigolds, use a dibber (dibble), cane or pencil to make holes for each seed. Plant the seeds and cover with compost.

2 When sowing small seeds they should be thinly scattered on the surface of the compost (soil mix) and then covered with just enough sieved sand and compost to conceal them. Firm the surface, using another tray. Water from above, using a fine rose on a watering-can, or by standing the tray in water until the surface of the compost is moist.

1 Remove the new soft-wood growth when it is about 10cm (4in) long, just above a leaf node.

3 Dip the end of the stem in hormone rooting powder, and plant up in a small container, using cuttings compost (soil mix).

2 Using a sharp knife, trim the cutting just below a node and trim away the lower leaves.

4 Fill the pot with cuttings, water, and place in a warm, bright place, out of scorching sunlight.

3 Enclose the seed tray in a plastic jar or bag to conserve moisture and cover with a black plastic bag, as most seeds germinate best in a warm dark place.

4 Check daily and bring into the light when the seedlings are showing.

5 To create a moist microclimate for the cuttings, it's a good idea to enclose the pot completely in a plastic bag. Secure it with an elastic band around the pot.

Mail Order

Send off each year for the latest seed and plant catalogues. You will invariably find a wider range than you can buy in a garden centre. Young plants are packed into special packages, which minimize damage during transit, but as they are restricted and in the dark they are initially weakened and some care is necessary to encourage vigorous growth.

1 Open the package with care. Leaves will probably unfold from the confined space. Each plant should be intact and clearly labelled.

2 Lift the plants out of their travelling box. Labels tucked underneath the root-ball reduce the necessity for handling it directly and helps to keep the compost (soil mix) intact.

3 Plant in a small pot. If the plants seem very wilted, remove some of the larger leaves.

Potting-On

After several weeks your young plants, whether grown from seed, mail order stock or cuttings, will need potting-on. This simply means giving the young plant its own larger, individual container.

1 Young plants are ready to move into larger pots when the roots start to emerge through the holes in the base of the pot. Gently remove the root-ball from the pot to check. If there is more than one seedling in the pot, carefully tease away each individual root-ball. (Some plants hate to have their roots disturbed. The information on the seed packet will tell you this. These seeds are best sown individually in peat pots or modular trays.) Lower the root-ball of the plant into a pot marginally bigger than the existing one.

2 Holding the plant carefully so as not to damage the stem, gently pour potting compost (soil mix) around the root-ball, firming lightly.

3 Dibble the compost (soil mix) down the side of the pot to eliminate air spaces. It does not matter if the stem of the seedling is buried deeper than it was previously, as long as the leaves are well clear of the soil. Water, using a can with a fine rose.

Choosing composts

Composts (soil mixes) come in various formulations to suit different plant requirements. A standard potting compost is usually peat-based and is suitable for all purposes. Peat and peat substitutes are relatively light in weight and therefore the best choice for hanging baskets. Regular watering is vital when using peat-based composts, as it is very difficult to moisten them again if they have been allowed to dry out completely. Different composts can be mixed together for specific plant needs.

Standard compost (soil mix)

The majority of composts available at garden centres are peat-based with added fertilizers.

Ericaceous compost

A peat-based compost with no added lime, essential for rhododendrons, camellias and heathers in containers.

Container compost

A peat-based compost with moisture-retaining granules and added fertilizer, specially formulated for windowboxes and containers.

Peat-free compost

Manufacturers now offer a range of composts using materials from renewable resources such as coir fibre. They are used in the same way as peat-based composts.

Loam-based compost

Uses sterilized loam as the main ingredient, with fertilizers to supplement the nutrients in the loam. Although much heavier than peat-based compost, it can be lightened by mixing with peat-free compost. Ideal for long-term planting as it retains nutrients well.

THE ESSENTIAL FERTILIZER ELEMENTS

All plant fertilizers contain three key elements, nitrogen (N), phosphorous (P), and potassium/potash (K), with extra trace elements. These three promote, respectively, foliage growth, flower development, and fruit ripening and root development.

When buying a packet of fertilizer you can easily check the balance of the ingredients. It is printed as an "NPK" ratio, for instance 12:5:12. But don't be fooled into thinking that a reading of 24:10:24 is stronger, giving twice the value. It won't, of course, as the ratio is the same. A fertilizer with a ratio of 10:5:10 provides a sound, balanced diet. (You can purchase meters from garden centres that give a guide to the nutrient levels in the soil but they are not, to date, particularly accurate.)

Besides feeding, you can also trick some plants into a prolific display of flowering. Plants packed into small containers, with restricted (but not crippling) root space, feel that they are in danger of dying. Their immediate response is to do what all flowering plants are programmed to do – flower and set seed to continue the species.

Feeding container plants

It is not generally understood that most potting composts (soil mixes) contain sufficient food for only six weeks of plant growth. After that, the plants will slowly starve unless more food is introduced. There are several products available, all of which are easy to use. Many of the projects in this book use slow-release plant food granules because they are the easiest and most reliable way of ensuring your plants receive sufficient food during the growing season. For these granules to be effective the compost needs to remain damp or the nutrients cannot be released.

Slow-release Plant Food Granules

These will keep your container plants in prime condition and are very easy to use. One application lasts six months, whereas most other plant foods need to be applied fortnightly. Follow the manufacturer's recommended dose carefully; additional fertilizer will simply leach away.

BELOW: *A variety of plant foods (clockwise from top left): liquid foliar feed, two types of pelleted slow-release plant food granules, a general fertilizer and loose slow-release plant food granules.*

TOP: *Slow-release plant food granules can be added to the compost (soil mix) in the recommended quantity before filling the container and planting it.*

ABOVE: *When adding fertilizer granules to the soil, sprinkle them on to the surface of the compost (soil mix) and rake into the top layer. Pelleted granules should be pushed approximately 2cm (³/₄in) below the surface.*

Watering container plants

Watering plants in containers is an acquired art, and an incredibly important one. You cannot leave it entirely to nature because rain tends to bounce off the leaves of the bushiest plants, soaking not into the pot but into the adjoining ground.

Outside, pot plants dry out very quickly on roasting hot days. Unlike plants in the ground, their roots are encircled by heat; some thirsty plants might even need two waterings a day, so keep checking. You have to get the balance right between over- and under-watering.

Trial and error is one way, but there are a few key tips, one of the best and simplest being to stick your finger deep into the soil to test for dryness. If you are unsure, wait until you see the first signs of wilting, then give the plant a thorough drink, letting the water drain out of the bottom of the pot. And always water plants either first thing in the morning or, better still, late at night, so that the moisture does not quickly evaporate. At all costs, try to avoid over-watering, which is a bigger killer than pests and diseases combined.

The best water is either rainwater or cold, boiled water, but it is not essential to use these unless your tap water is very hard, or you are growing lime-hating plants such as camellias. Don't allow your

potted plants to become waterlogged. If there is any water remaining in the saucer half an hour after watering, tip it away.

Windowboxes and Pots

Don't rush the watering. Though you might think one soaking is enough for a big window box, it might only wet the top layer of compost (soil mix). Wait until the water sluices out of the bottom. Container composts include a water-retaining gel and if the compost remains wet in cold weather it can cause the roots to rot.

Hanging Baskets

Summer hanging baskets need daily watering even in overcast weather and on a hot day should be watered morning and evening. Once they have been allowed to dry out it can be difficult for the compost (soil mix) to re-absorb water. In these circumstances it is a good idea to immerse hanging baskets in a large bucket or bowl of water. Winter and spring hanging baskets should be watered only when the soil is dry.

LEFT: *Houseplants enjoy being sprayed with water, but in hard water areas you should use rainwater or bottled water.*

Water-retaining Gel

One of the main problems for most container gardeners is the amount of watering required to keep the plants thriving in the growing season. Adding water-retaining gels to compost (soil mix) will certainly help reduce this task. Sachets of gel are available from garden centres.

1 Pour the recommended amount of water into a bowl.

2 Scatter the gel over the surface, stirring occasionally until it has absorbed the water.

3 Add to your compost (soil mix) at the recommended rate, and mix the gel in thoroughly before using it for planting.

MULCHES

A mulch is a layer of protective material placed over the soil. It helps to retain moisture, conserve warmth, suppress weeds and prevent soil splash on foliage and flowers.

Bark chippings

Bark is an extremely effective mulch and as it rots down it conditions the soil. It works best when spread at least 7.5cm (3in) thick and is therefore not ideal for small containers. It is derived from renewable resources.

Clay granules

Clay granules are widely used for hydroculture, but can also be used to mulch houseplants. When placing a plant in a *cachepot*, fill all around the pot with granules. When watered, the granules absorb moisture, which is then released slowly to create a moist microclimate for the plant.

Gravel

Gravel makes a decorative mulch for container plants, and also provides the correct environment for plants such as alpines. It is available in a variety of sizes and colours which can be matched to the scale and colours of the plants used.

Stones

Smooth stones can be used as decorative mulch for large container-grown plants. You can save stones dug out of the garden or buy stones from garden centres. They also deter cats from using the soil as a litter tray.

Pests and diseases

Container plants are every bit as susceptible to aphid and slug attacks as those grown in the garden. But they are generally easier to keep an eye on, so the moment you see a pest attack, take action. Most pests multiply at a staggering rate, and once a plant has been vigorously assaulted, it takes a long time to recover.

Common Pests

Aphids

These sap-sucking insects feed on the tender growing tips. Most insecticides are effective against aphids such as greenfly or blackfly (shown above). Choose one that will not harm ladybirds.

Mealy bugs

These look like spots of white mould. They are hard to shift and regular treatment with a systemic insecticide is the best solution.

Caterpillars

The occasional caterpillar can be picked off the plant and disposed of as you see fit, but a major infestation can strip a plant before your eyes. Contact insecticides are usually very effective.

Red spider mite

An insect that thrives indoors in dry conditions. Constant humidity will reduce the chance of an infestation, which is indicated by the presence of fine webs and mottling of the plant's leaves. To treat an infestation, pick off the worst affected leaves and spray the plants with an insecticide.

Vine weevils

These white grubs are a menace. The first sign of an infestation is the sudden collapse of the plant because the weevil has eaten its roots. Systemic insecticides or natural predators can be used as a preventative, but once a plant has been attacked it is usually too late to save it. Never re-use the soil from an affected plant. The picture above shows an adult weevil.

Snails

Snails cannot generally reach hanging baskets, but are more of a problem in wall baskets and windowboxes: they tuck themselves behind the container during daylight and venture out to feast at night. Use slug pellets or venture out yourself with a torch (flashlight) and catch them.

Whitefly

These tiny white flies flutter up in clouds when disturbed from their feeding places on the undersides of leaves. Whitefly are particularly troublesome in conservatories, where a dry atmosphere will encourage them to breed. Keep the air as moist as possible. Contact insecticides will need more than one application to deal with an infestation, but a systemic insecticide will protect the plant for weeks.

Common Diseases

Black spot – most commonly seen on roses; dark spots on leaves occur before they fall. Burn all affected foliage, and treat with a fungicide.
Botrytis – immediately evident as a pernicious, furry grey mould. Remove and burn all affected parts, and treat with a fungicide.
Powdery mildew – most likely to affect potted fruit trees. Remove and burn affected parts. Treat with a fungicide.
Rust – high humidity causes orange/dark brown pustules on the stem. Remove and burn affected parts. Treat with a fungicide.
Viruses (various) – the varied symptoms include distorted, mis-shapen leaves, and discoloration. Vigorous anti-aphid controls are essential. Destroy affected foliage.

Pest Control

There are three main types of pest control available to combat common pests.

Systemic insecticides

These work by being absorbed by the plant's root or leaf system, and killing insects that come into contact with the plant. This will work for difficult pests, such as the grubs of vine weevils which are hidden in the soil, and scale insects which protect themselves from above with a scaly cover.

Contact insecticides

These must be sprayed directly on to the insects to be effective. Most organic insecticides work this way, but they generally kill all insects, even beneficial ones, such as hoverflies and ladybirds. Try to remove these before spraying the infected plant.

Biological control

Commercial growers now use biological control in their glasshouses; this means natural predators are introduced to eat the pest population. Although not all are suitable for the amateur gardener, they can be used in conservatories for dealing with pests such as whitefly.

NATURAL PREDATORS

Aphidius – a wasp that lays eggs in young aphids; on hatching they devour the host.
Aphidoletes – a gall midge that devours aphids.
Bacillus thuringinesis – a bacterium that kills caterpillars.
Cryptolaemus montrouzieri – an Australian ladybird that eats mealy bug. It is activated by a temperature of 20°C (68°F).
Encarsia formosa – a parasitic wasp that lays eggs in the larvae of whitefly. The young wasps eat their hosts.

Metaphycus – a parasitic wasp, activated by a temperature of 20°C (68°F), that kills off soft scales.
Phasmarhabditis – a nematode that kills slugs provided the temperature of the soil is above 5°C (41°F).
Phytoseiulus persimilis – attacks red spider mite provided the temperature is 20°C (68°F).
Steinernema – kills vine weevils by releasing a bacterium into them. Needs a temperature of 12°C (53°F).

Spring Containers

*I*n the autumn thoughts turn to planting for the new year. Bulbs are always a popular choice to welcome spring and if planted in layers will give you a second display too.

Small containers of spring flowers brighten up a patio, and a tub of daffodils and wallflowers provides a colourful arrangement in the garden. Pots of yellow daffodils, tulips and pansies arranged in a container give an instant display of spring flowers and when flowering is over, the pots of bulbs can be tucked away in a corner of the garden to flower again next year.

Spring into action

On misty, autumn days spring might seem a long time away, but gardeners have to think ahead. If you want a cheerful pot of flowers to greet you early next year, now is the time to get planting. There are hundreds of different types of spring-flowering bulbs to choose from, and mixed and matched with forget-me-nots, daisies, pansies or wallflowers, you cannot go wrong.

MATERIALS

Large flower pot
Small stones
Compost (soil mix)

PLANTS

Tulip bulbs
Wallflowers
  (cheiranthus)
Forget-me-nots,
  daisies or
  pansies (violas)

FORGET-ME-NOT

TULIP BULBS

WALLFLOWERS

GARDENER'S TIP

The plants will not need heavy watering over the autumn and winter, but they will need an occasional drink so keep an eye on the pot in case it dries out.

PLANT IN AUTUMN

1 Use a large container and put a few stones over the hole in the bottom for drainage. Fill the pot two-thirds full with compost (soil mix).

2 Plant about 5 tulip bulbs. Cover the bulbs with handfuls of compost (soil mix).

3 Using your hands to make holes, plant three wallflowers evenly spaced out. If you dig up a tulip bulb by mistake, just pop it back in again.

4 Fill any gaps with forget-me-nots, daisies or pansies, or a mixture. Give all the plants a good watering.

Daffodils and wallflowers

A weathered wooden tub planted in the autumn with daffodil bulbs and wallflower plants will provide a colourful spring display. Alternatively, you can buy pots of daffodils and wallflowers in bud in the early spring and plant them for an instant show.

MATERIALS

36cm (14in) wooden tub
Polystyrene or other drainage material
Compost (soil mix)
Slow-release plant food granules

PLANTS

24 daffodil bulbs or 4 1-litre (5in) pots of daffodils
3 bushy wallflower (Cheiranthus) plants

DAFFODIL

WALLFLOWER

GARDENER'S TIP

To save the bulbs for next year, allow the leaves to die right back and then dig up and store in a cool dry place.

PLANT BULBS IN THE AUTUMN OR PLANTS IN BUD IN SPRING

1 Break the polystyrene (plastic foam) into large pieces and fill the bottom third of the tub to provide drainage and to save on the quantity of compost (soil mix) used.

2 Add compost (soil mix) until the tub is half-full and arrange 12 of the daffodil bulbs evenly over the surface. Cover the bulbs with compost.

3 Arrange the remaining 12 bulbs on the surface of the compost (soil mix). Remove the wallflower plants from their pots and place on the compost. Don't worry if the plants cover some of the bulbs, they will grow round the wallflowers. Fill the tub with compost, pressing down firmly around the wallflowers to ensure that they do not work loose in windy weather. Sprinkle a tablespoon of plant food granules on to the surface and work into the top layer of compost.

Miniature spring garden

Terracotta pots filled with crocuses, irises and primroses nestling in a bed of moss, make a delightful scaled-down spring garden which would fit on the smallest balcony or even a window-sill.

IRIS

MOSS

CROCUS

PRIMROSE

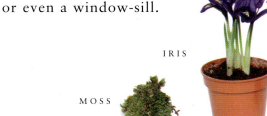

MATERIALS

Terracotta seed tray
2 terracotta pots, 13cm (5in) high
Crocks (broken pots)
Compost (soil mix)
Bun moss

PLANTS

3 primroses
Pot of Iris reticulata
Pot of crocuses

1 Cover the drainage holes of the seed tray and the two pots with crocks (broken pots).

2 Half-fill the seed tray with compost (soil mix). Before planting the primroses, loosen the roots by gently squeezing the root-ball and teasing the roots loose.

3 Arrange the primroses in the seed tray and fill with compost (soil mix) around the plants, pressing down around the plants to ensure they are firmly planted.

4 Arrange the bun moss around the plants so that all the compost (soil mix) is hidden.

5 Remove the irises from their plastic pot and slip them into a terracotta pot. Bed them in with a little extra compost (soil mix) if necessary, and then arrange moss around the base of the stems.

6 Repeat this process with the crocuses and then water all the containers and arrange them together.

GARDENER'S TIP

Once the irises and crocuses are past their best, hide them behind other pots to die down and dry out before starting them into growth again in the autumn.

PLANT IN EARLY SPRING

Spring flowers in an instant

An arrangement of pots of spring flowers is surrounded with bark to give the appearance of a planted windowbox. As soon as the flowers are over, the pots can be removed and left to die back, and the container is ready for its summer planting.

MATERIALS

40cm (16in) terracotta
 windowbox
Bark chippings

PLANTS

Pot of daffodils
Pot of yellow tulips
4 yellow pansies
 in pots

DAFFODIL

PANSY

TULIP

GARDENER'S TIP

Once the flowers have finished and the pots have been removed from the windowbox, the pots of bulbs can be tucked away in a corner of the garden ready to flower again next year.

PLANT IN LATE WINTER OR EARLY SPRING

1 Position the pot of daffodils at the right-hand end of the windowbox.

2 Position the pot of tulips at the left-hand end of the windowbox.

3 Fill the centre and around the pots with bark chippings until the windowbox is half-full.

4 Position the pansies between the tulips and the daffodils, and add bark until all the pots are concealed. Water moderately and stand in any position.

A spring display of auriculas

An old strawberry punnet carrier makes an attractive and unusual windowbox in which to display some beautifully marked auriculas planted in antique terracotta pots. A large flower basket or wooden trug would look just as good as this marvellous old wooden carrier.

MATERIALS

8 8–10cm (3–4in) old or antique-style terracotta pots
Crocks (broken pots) or other suitable drainage material
Compost (soil mix)
50cm (20in) wooden carrier

PLANTS

8 different auriculas (Primula auricula)

AURICULAS

GARDENER'S TIP

A window-sill is an ideal position to see auriculas at their best. It is difficult to admire the full drama of their markings if they are at ground level. When they have finished flowering, stand the pots in a shady corner or a cold frame.

PLANT IN EARLY SPRING

1 Place a crock over the drainage hole of a pot.

2 Remove an auricula from its plastic pot and plant it firmly with added compost (soil mix).

3 Stand the newly planted auricula in the wooden carrier.

4 Repeat the process for the other plants to fill the carrier. Water thoroughly and stand in light shade.

Display in a copper tub

A battered old washing boiler makes an attractive and characterful container for a display of white tulips, underplanted with purple violets and evergreen periwinkles.

MATERIALS

60cm (24in) copper boiler
20cm (8in) plastic pot
Compost (soil mix)

PLANTS

20 white tulip bulbs
  or tulips in bud
5 purple violets
2 periwinkles
  (Vinca minor)

VIOLET

TULIP

PERIWINKLE

GARDENER'S TIP

Lift the tulips when they have finished flowering and hang them up to dry in a cool airy place. They can be replanted late in autumn to flower again next year. Provided you pick off the dead heads, the violets will flower all summer. For a summer display, lift the central violet and plant a standard white marguerite in the centre of the container.

PLANT BULBS IN AUTUMN OR PLANTS IN BUD IN SPRING. PLANT THE VIOLETS AND PERIWINKLES IN SPRING

1 Place the upturned plastic pot in the base of the tub before filling it with compost (soil mix). This will save on the amount of compost used, and will not have any effect on the growth of the plants as they will still have plenty of room for their roots.

3 Do the underplanting in early spring. The compost (soil mix) will have settled in the container and should be topped up to within 7.5cm (3in) of the rim. Remove the violets from their pots. Gently tweak the root-balls and loosen the roots to aid the plants' growth.

5 Plant a periwinkle on either side of the central violet, again loosening the root-balls.

2 If you are planting tulip bulbs, half-fill the container with compost (soil mix), arrange the bulbs evenly over the surface and then cover them with a good 15cm (6in) of compost. This should be done in late autumn.

4 Plant one violet in the centre and four around the edges. Scoop out the soil by hand to avoid damaging the growing tips of the tulips beneath the surface.

6 If you are planting tulips in bud, the whole scheme should be planted at the same time, interplanting the tulips with the violets and periwinkles. Position in sun or partial shade.

Scented spring planter

Lilies-of-the-valley grow very well in containers and they will thrive in the shade where their delicate scented flowers stand out amongst the greenery. Surrounding the plants with bun moss is practical as well as attractive as it will stop the soil splashing back on to the leaves and flowers during fierce spring showers.

MATERIALS

Tinware planter
Clay granules
Compost
   (soil mix)
Bun moss

PLANTS

6–8 pots of lily-of-the-valley

LILY OF THE VALLEY

1 Fill the bottom of the planter with 5cm (2in) of clay granules to improve drainage.

2 Cover the granules with a layer of compost (soil mix) and arrange the lily-of-the-valley plants evenly on the compost.

3 Fill in around the plants with more compost (soil mix), making sure to press firmly around the plants so that they won't rock about in the wind. Now cover the compost with bun moss, fitting it snugly around the stems of the lily-of-the-valley, as this will also help keep the plants upright.

GARDENER'S TIP

If you want to bring your planter indoors to enjoy the scent of the flowers, use a container without drainage holes in the base, but be very careful not to overwater. Once the plants have finished flowering replant them in a pot with normal drainage holes or in the garden. They are woodland plants and will be quite happy under trees.

PLANT IN EARLY SPRING

Woodland garden

You do not need your own woodland area for this garden, just a shady corner and an attractive container to hold a selection of plants that thrive in damp shade. The plants are buried in bark chippings in their pots and will relish these conditions as they closely imitate their natural habitat.

MATERIALS

50cm (20in) glazed pot
Bark chippings

FERNS

BLUEBELL

ANEMONE
BLANDA

PLANTS

Pot of bluebells
3 hardy ferns
Pot of Anemone blanda

1 Fill the container three-quarters full with bark chippings. Plant your largest pot (in this case the bluebells) first. Scoop a hollow in the bark and position the pot so that the base of the leaves is approximately 5cm (2in) below the rim of the container.

2 Cover the pot with bark so that the plastic is no longer visible and the plant is surrounded by chippings.

3 Arrange the ferns so that they relate attractively to one another. Fill the spaces between the ferns with bark.

4 Add the *Anemone blanda* at the front of the container where its flowers will be seen to best advantage, and then top up the whole arrangement with bark. Stand the container in light shade and water.

GARDENER'S TIP

After the bluebells and anemones have finished flowering, lift them out of the container in their pots and set them aside in a shady corner to rest. They can be replaced by other woodland plants such as wild strawberries or periwinkle.

PLANT IN EARLY SPRING

A garland of spring flowers

Miniature daffodils, deep blue pansies, yellow polyanthus and variegated ivy are planted together to make a hanging basket that will flower for many weeks in early spring, lifting the spirits with its fresh colours and delicate woodland charm.

MATERIALS

30cm (12in) hanging basket
Sphagnum moss
Compost (soil mix)
Slow-release plant food granules

PLANTS

3 variegated ivies
5 miniature daffodil bulbs 'Tête-à-Tête' or similar, or a pot of daffodils in bud
3 blue pansies
2 yellow polyanthus

POLYANTHUS

IVY

PANSY

MINIATURE DAFFODIL

1 Line the lower half of the basket with moss.

3 Line the rest of the basket with moss and add a layer of compost (soil mix) to the bottom of the basket. Push the daffodil bulbs into the compost.

5 Plant the polyanthus between the pansies. Water the basket and hang in sun or shade. If planting daffodils in bud, remove them from the pot and place in the centre of the basket before arranging the ivies and filling with compost (soil mix).

2 Plant the ivies into the side of the basket by resting the root-balls on the moss, and guiding the foliage through the basket so that it will trail down.

4 Fill the remainder of the basket with compost (soil mix), working a teaspoon of slow-release plant food granules into the top layer. Plant the pansies, evenly spaced, in the top of the basket.

GARDENER'S TIP

When dismantling the arrangement, plant the variegated ivies in the garden. They look particularly good tumbling over walls, or threading their way through and linking established shrubs. Prune hard if they get out of hand and become too invasive.

PLANT IN AUTUMN IF GROWING DAFFODILS FROM BULBS; IN LATE WINTER OR EARLY SPRING FOR READY-GROWN DAFFODILS

Summer Containers

Summer is the highlight of the gardening year and containers can be used to create those extra colourful effects or even for creative plantings in themselves

A dark green or black windowbox makes a cool foil for the vibrant colour of shocking pink petunias and verbenas, and sweet-smelling summer flowers are combined with heliotrope and petunias to make a fragrant and visually pleasing display.

Keep watering as the flowers grow and remember that on hot days containers and baskets can dry out very quickly.

A wild one

Native plants are those that have grown naturally in the countryside for thousands of years. Some of the most colourful ones are cornfield flowers, but many are quite rare now. To enjoy them this summer, sow a pot full of wild flowers to stand on your doorstep.

MATERIALS

Pebbles
Very large flower pot
Garden soil

PLANTS

Packet of wild flower seeds

FLOWER
POT

WILD FLOWER
SEEDS

PEBBLES

GARDEN SOIL

1 Put a few pebbles in the base of the pot for drainage.

2 Fill the pot with garden soil, taking out any bits of roots or large stones.

3 Make sure the surface is level, then sprinkle a large pinch of flower seeds evenly on top.

4 Cover the seeds lightly with soil, just so you can't see them any more, and water them in with a gentle sprinkle.

GARDENER'S TIP

Remember to keep watering as the flowers grow!
Pots need much more watering than beds because the water drains away.

PLANT IN EARLY SPRING

A cottage terracotta planter

Charming, cottage-garden plants tumble from this terracotta windowbox in a colourful display. The sunny flowers of the nemesias, marigolds and nasturtiums mingle with the cool, soft green helichrysums and blue-green nasturtium leaves.

MATERIALS

36cm (14in) terracotta windowbox
Crocks (broken pots) or other suitable drainage material
Compost (soil mix)
Slow-release plant food granules

PLANTS

3 pot marigolds (calendulas)
2 Helichrysum petiolare 'Aureum'
2 nasturtiums
2 Nemesia 'Orange Prince'

MARIGOLD

HELICHRYSUM

NASTURTIUM

NEMESIAS

1 Cover the base of the container with crocks (broken pots) and fill with compost (soil mix), adding 2 teaspoons of plant food granules. Plant the marigolds along the back.

2 Plant the two helichrysums in the front corners of the windowbox.

3 Plant the nasturtiums between the marigolds at the back of the container.

4 Plant the nemesias between the helichrysums. Water well and stand in partial sun.

GARDENER'S TIP

The golden-leaved helichrysum retains a better colour if it is not in full sun all day. Too much sun makes it looks rather bleached.

PLANT IN SPRING

A miniature cottage garden

This basket derives its charm from its simple planting scheme. Pot marigolds and parsley are planted with bright blue felicias to create a basket which would look at home on the wall of a cottage or outside the kitchen door.

FELICIA

PARSLEY

POT
MARIGOLDS

MATERIALS

36cm (14in) hanging basket
Sphagnum moss
Compost (soil mix)
Slow-release plant food granules

PLANTS

5 parsley plants
3 pot marigolds (Calendula 'Gitana', or similar)
3 felicias

1 Line the lower half of the basket with moss.

2 Plant the parsley into the sides of the basket by resting the root-balls on the moss, and gently feeding the foliage through the wires.

3 Line the rest of the basket with moss, carefully tucking it around the roots of the parsley.

4 Fill the basket with compost (soil mix), mixing a teaspoon of slow-release plant food granules into the top layer.

5 Plant the three pot marigolds, evenly spaced, in the top of the basket.

6 Plant the felicias between the marigolds. Water well and hang in full or partial sun.

GARDENER'S TIP

Regular dead-heading will keep the basket looking good, but allow at least one of the marigold flowers to form a seedhead and you will be able to grow your own plants next year.

PLANT IN SPRING

Full of cheer

Vivid red pelargoniums and verbenas are combined with cheerful yellow bidens and soft green helichrysums in this planter, which brightens the exterior of an old barn.

MATERIALS

76cm (30in) plastic windowbox
Compost (soil mix)
Slow-release plant food granules

PLANTS

3 scarlet pelargoniums
2 Bidens ferulifolia
2 yellow trailing verbenas
2 Helichrysum petiolare 'Aureum'

HELICHRYSUM

PELARGONIUM

BIDENS

VERBENA

GARDENER'S TIP

Regular dead-heading and an occasional foliar feed will keep the pelargoniums flowering prolifically all summer.

PLANT IN SPRING

1 The easiest way to make drainage holes in a plastic planter is with an electric drill.

2 Fill the windowbox with compost (soil mix), working in 2 teaspoons of slow-release plant food granules.

3 Plant the pelargoniums, evenly spaced, in the windowbox.

4 Plant the two bidens on either side of the central pelargonium to spill over the front of the planter.

5 Plant the two verbenas on either side of the central pelargonium towards the back of the planter.

6 Plant the helichrysums in the front corners. Water thoroughly and stand the box in a sunny position.

A trough of alpines

A selection of easy-to-grow alpine plants is grouped in a basket-weave stone planter to create a miniature garden. The mulch of gravel is both attractive and practical as it prevents soil splashing on to the leaves of the plants.

MATERIALS

40cm (16in) stone trough
Crocks (broken pots)
Compost (soil mix)
Slow-release plant food granules
Gravel

PLANTS

Sempervivum
Alpine aquilegia
White rock rose (helianthemum)
Papaver alpinum
Alpine phlox
Pink saxifrage
White saxifrage

PAPAVER ALPINUM

SEMPERVIVUM

SAXIFRAGES

ALPINE PHLOX

ROCK ROSE

ALPINE AQUILEGIA

1 Cover the base of the trough with crocks (broken pots). Fill the container with compost (soil mix), working in a teaspoon of plant food granules and extra gravel for improved drainage.

2 Arrange the plants, still in their pots, in the trough to decide on the most attractive arrangement. Complete the planting, working across the trough.

3 Scatter a good layer of gravel around the plants. Water thoroughly and stand in a sunny position.

GARDENER'S TIP

Tidy the trough once a month, removing dead flowerheads and leaves, adding more gravel if necessary. A trough like this will last a number of years before it needs replanting.

PLANT IN SPRING

Delicate summer flowers

CONVOLVULUS

BRACHYCOME

PANSIES

Pale orange pansies contrast beautifully with the lavender-blue convolvulus, and the pastel yellow brachycome daisies link the whole scheme together.

MATERIALS

30cm (12in) hanging basket
Sphagnum moss
Compost (soil mix)
Slow-release plant food granules

PLANTS

3 orange pansies
3 Brachycome 'Lemon Mist'
2 Convolvulus sabatius

1 Line the basket with moss and fill with compost, mixing a teaspoon of slow-release plant food granules into the top layer. Plant the pansies around the edge.

2 Plant the brachycome daisies between the pansies.

3 Place the convolvulus plants in the centre of the basket so that the tendrils can weave between the other plants. Water and hang in full or partial sun.

GARDENER'S TIP

Each time you water this basket be sure to remove any pansy flowers that are past their best. Once pansies start to set seed they quickly grow leggy and stop flowering.

PLANT IN SPRING

A mass of sweet peas

This large basket is filled with sweet peas surrounding a regal pelargonium. It is inter-planted with chives to provide a contrasting leaf shape and help deter pests. Their fluffy purple flowers will add a further dimension to the arrangement, and the leaves can be snipped off for use in the kitchen.

MATERIALS

40cm (16in) hanging basket
Sphagnum moss
Compost (soil mix)
Slow-release plant food granules

PLANTS

Regal Pelargonium 'Sancho Panza'
2–3 small pots or a strip of low-growing sweet peas such as 'Snoopea'
3 chive plants

SWEET PEAS

CHIVES

PELARGONIUM

1 Line the basket with a generous layer of moss.

2 Fill the basket with compost (soil mix) and work a teaspoon of slow-release plant food granules into the top layer. Plant the regal pelargonium in the centre of the basket.

3 Gently divide the sweet peas into clumps of about eight plants each.

4 Plant the sweet pea clumps around the edge of the basket.

5 Plant the chives between the sweet peas and the central pelargonium.

6 Fill any gaps with more moss. Water well and hang the basket in a sunny position.

GARDENER'S TIP

Sweet peas will bloom longer if you keep picking the flowers and be sure to remove any seed pods as they form. Similarly, the chives grow longer and are stronger if their flowerheads are removed before they seed.

PLANT IN LATE SPRING

Hot flowers in a cool container

Shocking-pink petunias and verbenas are the dominant plants in this windowbox which also features a softer pink marguerite and silver helichrysum. Either a dark green, or black-painted wooden windowbox provides a pleasing foil for the vibrant flowers.

MATERIALS

76cm (30in) plastic windowbox with drainage holes
90cm (3ft) wooden windowbox (optional)
Compost (soil mix)
Slow-release plant food granules

PLANTS

Trailing pink marguerite (Argyranthemum 'Flamingo')
2 bright pink verbenas, such as 'Sissinghurst'
3 shocking-pink petunias
4 Helichrysum petiolare microphyllum

MARGUERITE

VERBENA

PETUNIA

HELICHRYSUM

GARDENER'S TIP

To add height to this scheme, buy some 30cm (12in) green plant sticks. Push two into the soil behind each of the verbenas, and train them upwards.

PLANT IN LATE SPRING OR EARLY SUMMER

1 Fill the plastic windowbox with compost (soil mix), adding in 3 teaspoons of slow-release plant food granules. Plant the marguerite centre front.

2 Plant the verbenas in the back corners of the windowbox.

3 Plant one of the petunias behind the marguerite, and the other two on either side of it.

4 Plant one helichrysum on each side of the central petunia, and the other two in the front corners of the windowbox. Water well and lift into place. Stand in a sunny position.

Sweet-smelling summer flowers

Scented pelargonium and verbena are combined with heliotrope and petunias to make a windowbox that is fragrant as well as a visual pleasure.

MATERIALS

40cm (16in) terracotta windowbox
Crocks (broken pots) or other suitable drainage material
Compost (soil mix)
Slow-release plant food granules

PLANTS

Scented-leaf Pelargonium *'Lady Plymouth'*
3 soft pink petunias
Heliotrope
2 Verbena 'Pink Parfait'

HELIOTROPE

PETUNIA

VERBENA

PELARGONIUM

GARDENER'S TIP

At the end of the summer the pelargonium can be potted up and kept through the winter as a houseplant. Reduce the height of the plant by at least a half and it will soon send out new shoots.

PLANT IN LATE SPRING OR EARLY SUMMER

1 Cover the base of the window-box with a layer of crocks (broken pots). Fill with compost (soil mix), working in 2 teaspoons of plant food granules. Plant the pelargonium to the right of centre, towards the back.

2 Plant a petunia in each corner and one in the centre at the front of the windowbox.

3 Plant the heliotrope to the left of the pelargonium.

4 Plant one verbena behind the heliotrope and the other in front of the pelargonium. Water well and place in a sunny position.

A basket of contrasts

The deep green and burgundy foliage of *Fuchsia* 'Thalia' will be even more startling later in summer when the bright red pendant flowers stand out against the leaves and compete with the glowing colours of the nemesias. The yellow-green helichrysums provide a cooling contrast.

MATERIALS

30cm (12in) wall basket
Sphagnum moss
Compost (soil mix)
Slow-release plant food granules

PLANTS

3 Helichrysum petiolare *'Aureum'*
Fuchsia *'Thalia'*
4 nemesias in red, yellow and orange tones

NEMESIA

HELICHRYSUM

FUCHSIA

GARDENER'S TIP

Dead-head the nemesias regularly to ensure that they continue flowering throughout the summer.

PLANT IN LATE SPRING OR EARLY SUMMER

1 Line the back of the basket and the lower half of the front with moss. Fill the lower half of the basket with compost (soil mix).

2 Plant two of the helichrysum plants into the side of the basket by resting the root-balls on the moss, and carefully feeding the foliage through the wires.

3 Line the rest of the basket with moss and top up with compost (soil mix). Work a half-teaspoon of slow-release plant food granules into the top layer. Plant the fuchsia in the centre.

4 Plant the remaining helichrysum in front of the fuchsia. Plant two nemesias on each side of the central plants. Water the basket well and hang in full or partial sun.

A space in the sun

Since osteospermum, portulaca and diascia are all sun-lovers this is definitely a basket for your sunniest spot, where the plants will thrive and the colours will look their best.

PORTULACA

DIASCIA

OSTEOSPERMUM

MATERIALS

36cm (14in) hanging basket
Sphagnum moss
Compost (soil mix)
Slow-release plant food granules

PLANTS

6 peach portulaca
Osteospermum *'Buttermilk'*
3 Diascia 'Salmon Supreme', or similar

1 Line the lower half of the basket with moss. Plant three portulaca by resting the root-balls on the moss, and guiding the foliage between the wires.

2 Add more moss to the basket, tucking it carefully around the portulaca.

3 Partly fill the basket with compost (soil mix). Work a teaspoon of plant food granules into the top layer. Plant the remaining three portulaca just below the rim of the basket.

4 Line the rest of the basket with moss. Plant the osteopermum centrally. Plant the diascias around the osteospermum. Water thoroughly and hang in a sunny spot.

GARDENER'S TIP

Keep pinching out the growing tips of the osteospermum to ensure a bushy plant.

PLANT IN LATE SPRING OR EARLY SUMMER

An antique wall basket

This old wirework basket is an attractive container for a planting scheme which includes deep pink pansies, a variegated ivy-leaved pelargonium with soft pink flowers, a blue convolvulus and deep pink alyssum.

MATERIALS

30cm (12in) wall basket
Sphagnum moss
Compost (soil mix)
Slow-release plant food granules

PLANTS

5 rose-pink alyssum
Pelargonium 'L'Elégante'
3 deep pink pansies
Convolvulus sabatius

ALYSSUM

PELARGONIUM

CONVOLVULUS

PANSY

GARDENER'S TIP

Wall baskets look good among climbing plants, but you will need to trim the surrounding foliage if it gets too exuberant.

PLANT IN LATE SPRING OR EARLY SUMMER

1 Line the back of the basket and the lower half of the front with moss. Plant the alyssum into the side by resting the root-balls on the moss, and guiding the foliage through the wires.

2 Line the remainder of the basket with moss and fill with compost (soil mix), working a half-teaspoon of plant food granules into the top layer. Plant the pelargonium at the front of the basket.

3 Plant the pansies around the pelargonium. Plant the convolvulus at the back of the basket, trailing its foliage through the other plants. Water well and hang in partial sun.

A lime-green and blue box

MATERIALS

*76cm (30in) plastic windowbox
  with drainage holes*
Compost (soil mix)
Slow-release plant food granules

PLANTS

5 lime-green tobacco plants
2 scaevola
2 Helichrysum petiolare *'Aureum'*
3 Convolvulus sabatius

Lime-green flowering tobacco and helichrysums contrast beautifully with the blue scaevolas and convolvulus in this windowbox of cool colours.

SCAEVOLA

HELICHRYSUM

TOBACCO

CONVOLVULUS

1 Fill the window box with compost (soil mix), working in 3 teaspoons of plant food granules. Plant the tobacco plants along the back of the windowbox.

2 Plant the two scaevolas approximately 10cm (4in) from each end, in front of the tobacco plants.

3 Plant the two helichrysums on either side of the centre of the windowbox next to the scaevolas.

4 Plant two of the convolvulus in the front corners of the box and the third in the centre front. Water thoroughly and position in light shade or partial sun.

GARDENER'S TIP

At the end of the season pot up the scaevolas and convolvulus. Cut right back and protect from frost.

PLANT IN LATE SPRING

A touch of gold

Yellow lantana and the yellow-flowered variegated-leaf nasturtium provide colour from early summer onwards, and later in the season the black-eyed Susan will be covered in eye-catching flowers. Hang this exuberant basket high on a sunny wall so that the trailing plants can make as much growth as they like.

NASTURTIUM

BLACK-EYED SUSAN

LANTANA

MATERIALS

30cm (12in) hanging basket
Sphagnum moss
Compost (soil mix)
Slow-release plant food granules

PLANTS

3 Alaska nasturtiums
Yellow lantana
3 black-eyed Susans (Thunbergia alata)

1 Line the lower half of the basket with moss.

2 Plant the nasturtiums into the side of the basket by resting the root-balls on the moss, and carefully guiding the leaves through the wires.

3 Line the rest of the basket with moss. Fill the basket with compost (soil mix), working a teaspoon of slow-release plant food granules into the top layer.

4 Plant the lantana in the centre of the basket.

5 Plant the black-eyed Susans around the lantana. Water well and hang in a sunny position.

GARDENER'S TIP

Save some of the nasturtium seeds for next year's baskets and pots – they are among the easiest of plants to grow and some of the seeds are quite likely to find their own way into nearby cracks and crevices.

PLANT IN LATE SPRING OR EARLY SUMMER

Daisy chains

The soft yellow of the marguerites' flowers is emphasized by combining them with yellow-leaved helichrysum and bright blue felicia in this summery basket.

MARGUERITE

HELICHRYSUM

FELICIA

MATERIALS

40cm (16in) hanging basket
Sphagnum moss
Compost (soil mix)
Slow-release plant food granules

PLANTS

3 variegated felicias
3 yellow marguerites
(argyranthemums)
3 Helichrysum petiolare 'Aureum'

GARDENER'S TIP

Pinch out the growing tips of the marguerites regularly to encourage bushy plants.

PLANT IN LATE SPRING OR EARLY SUMMER

1 Line the lower half of the basket with moss. Plant the felicias into the sides of the basket by resting the root-balls on the moss, and carefully guiding the foliage through the wires.

2 Line the rest of the basket with moss. Fill with compost (soil mix), working a teaspoon of plant food granules into the top layer. Plant the marguerites in the top of the basket.

3 Plant the helichrysums between the marguerites, angling the plants to encourage them to grow over the edge of the basket. Water well and hang in full or partial sun.

A pastel composition

Pure white pelargonium blooms emerge from a sea of blue felicias, pinky-blue brachycome daisies and verbenas in this romantic basket.

PELARGONIUM

MATERIALS

36cm (14in) hanging basket
Sphagnum moss
Compost (soil mix)
Slow-release plant food granules

PLANTS

2 pink verbenas
2 Brachycome 'Pink Mist'
Blue felicia
White pelargonium

VERBENA

BRACHYCOME

FELICIA

1 Line the basket with moss and fill with compost (soil mix). Work a teaspoon of plant food granules into the top layer.

2 Plant the verbenas opposite each other at the edge of the basket, so that the foliage will tumble over the sides.

3 Plant the brachycome daisies around the edge of the basket. Plant the felicia off-centre in the middle of the basket.

4 Plant the pelargonium off-centre in the remaining space in the middle of the basket. Water thoroughly and hang in a sunny position.

GARDENER'S TIP

White pelargonium flowers discolour as they age; be sure to pick them off to keep the basket looking at its best.

PLANT IN LATE SPRING OR EARLY SUMMER

Fire and earth

The earth tones of this small decorative terracotta window-box are topped with the fiery reds and oranges of the plants – the fuchsia with its orange foliage and tubular scarlet flowers, the orange nasturtiums and the red claw-like flowers of the feathery-leaved lotus.

MATERIALS

36cm (14in) terracotta windowbox
Clay granules or other suitable drainage material
Compost (soil mix)
Slow-release plant food granules

PLANTS

Fuchsia *'Thalia'*
3 orange nasturtiums
2 Lotus berthelotii

NASTURTIUM

LOTUS

FUCHSIA

1 Cover the base of the window-box with drainage material. Fill with compost (soil mix) and a teaspoon of plant food granules.

2 Plant the fuchsia in the centre of the windowbox.

3 Plant the nasturtiums along the back of the windowbox.

4 Plant the two lotuses in the front of the windowbox on either side of the fuchsia. Water thoroughly, leave to drain, and stand in a sunny position.

GARDENER'S TIP

This stunning fuchsia is worth keeping for next year.
Pot it up in the autumn, cut back by half and overwinter on a window-sill or in a heated greenhouse.

PLANT IN LATE SPRING OR EARLY SUMMER

Wild strawberry basket

Wild strawberries can be grown in a basket and enjoyed anywhere, whether in the countryside or a small city garden.

MATERIALS

30cm (12in) square wire basket
Sphagnum moss
Equal mix loam-based compost (soil mix) and container compost
Slow-release plant food granules or organic plant food

PLANTS

4 alpine strawberry plants

ALPINE STRAWBERRY

1 Line the base and sides of the basket with a generous layer of sphagnum moss.

2 Fill the lined area with compost (soil mix). Scoop out a hollow for each strawberry plant, and firm the compost around the root-ball as you plant.

3 Scatter a tablespoon of plant food granules on the surface of the compost (soil mix).

4 Tuck more moss around the edges and under the leaves to conserve moisture and stop the fruit touching the soil. Water and place in full or partial sun.

GARDENER'S TIP

Propagate strawberry runners by pinning the plantlets into small pots of compost (soil mix). A loop of wire or a hairpin placed on either side of the plantlet will hold it firmly in place until it has rooted. Then simply cut the runner and you have a new strawberry plant.

PLANT IN SPRING TO FRUIT IN SUMMER

Autumn Containers

Use autumnal colours to announce the arrival of the season. Grow one or two autumn glory shrubs in tubs that you can bring out for a burst of colour on the patio.

Fuchsias flower prolifically into the autumn. The variegated foliage of 'Tom West', a hardy fuchsia, develops a rich pink colouring when grown in a sunny position and when underplanted with variegated ivies makes a stunning show. If the other plants in the container begin to look straggly, cut them right back and give them a liquid feed to give them renewed vigour.

Standard fuchsia

Fuchsia 'Tom West' is an excellent hardy variety that flowers well into autumn. Here, underplanted with variegated ivy, and benefiting from the large Chinese-style glazed pot, the display has a very modern chic appeal.

MATERIALS

Large glazed pot, at least 70cm (28in) diameter
Crocks (broken pots)
Peat-free compost (soil mix)
Slow-release plant food granules

PLANTS

1 half-standard Fuchsia 'Tom West'
6 variegated ivies

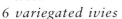
FUCHSIA

IVY

1 Cover the drainage hole in the base of the pot with the crocks (broken pots). This prevents it from becoming blocked and facilitates the free drainage of excess water.

2 Almost fill the pot with peat-free compost (soil mix). Add slow-release plant food granules to the compost.

3 Remove the half-standard fuchsia from its pot, and lower it gently on to the compost so that the top of its root-ball is slightly lower than the lip of the pot.

4 Add more compost (soil mix). Plant the variegated ivies around the base of the fuchsia. Fill in the gaps between the root-balls, and tease the ivies' stems and foliage across the compost surface. Water to settle the compost.

GARDENER'S TIP

The variegated foliage of 'Tom West' develops a lovely rich pink colouring when grown in a sunny position. The best foliage colour is on the young growth, so regular pinching out of new stem tips will ensure a colourful plant.

PLANT IN EARLY SPRING OR EARLY SUMMER

Foliage basket

This basket of evergreen foliage plants looks good all year round. The different leaf shapes and colours are emphasized when they are grouped together. Including flowers would detract from the architectural quality of the plants.

MATERIALS

30cm (12in) basket
Sphagnum moss
Loam-based compost (soil mix)
Slow-release plant food granules
Bark chippings

PLANTS

Phormium tenax
Mexican orange blossom
(Choisya ternata)
Carex brunnea '*Variegata*'

CAREX

PHORMIUM

MEXICAN ORANGE BLOSSOM

GARDENER'S TIP

A planted basket makes an ideal gift for a friend, especially when you have chosen the plants yourself. Include a label, giving the names of the plants and how to care for them.

PLANT AT ANY TIME OF THE YEAR

1 Line the basket with moss. Place the phormium at the back and position the orange blossom next to it.

2 Add the carex and fill between the plants with compost (soil mix) enriched with a tablespoon of slow-release plant food granules.

3 Mulch around the plants with bark chippings. Water well and place in partial shade.

Begonias and fuchsias

Fuchsias are wonderful hanging basket plants as they flower prolifically late into the autumn. By the end of summer, when the other plants may start to look a bit straggly, the fuchsia will be at its best with a glorious display of colour.

MATERIALS

36cm (14in) hanging basket
Sphagnum moss
Compost (soil mix)
Slow-release plant
    food granules

PLANTS

2 Diascia 'Ruby Field'
3 Helichrysum microphyllum
Fuchsia 'Rose Winston' or
    similar soft pink
3 deep pink begonias

BEGONIA

DIASCIA

HELICHRYSUM

FUCHSIA

1 Line the lower half of the basket with moss and arrange the diascias and helichrysums in the basket to decide where to plant each one. Ensure they do not become tangled in the wires.

2 Plant the two diascias into the sides of the basket by resting the root-balls in the moss, and gently feeding the foliage through the wires.

GARDENER'S TIP

If some of the plants in the basket begin to look straggly in comparison with the fuchsia, cut them right back and give a liquid feed – they will grow with renewed vigour and provide a wonderful autumn show.

PLANT IN LATE SPRING OR EARLY SUMMER

3 Line the rest of the basket with moss, partly fill with compost (soil mix) and plant the three helichrysums into the side of the basket near the rim.

4 Fill the basket with compost (soil mix). Work a teaspoon of plant food granules into the top layer of compost. Plant the fuchsia in the centre of the basket.

5 Finally, plant the three begonias around the fuchsia. Water well and hang the basket in full sun or partial shade.

Pot of sunflowers

Sunflowers grow very well in pots provided you are not growing the giant varieties. Grow your own from seed; there are many kinds to choose from, including the one with double flowers used here.

MATERIALS

30cm (12in) glazed pot
Polystyrene (plastic foam) or similar drainage material
Equal mix loam-based compost (soil mix) and container compost
Slow-release plant food granules

PLANTS

3 strong sunflower seedlings, approximately 20cm (8in) tall

SUNFLOWER SEEDLING

GARDENER'S TIP

Allow at least one of the sunflower heads to set seed. As the plant starts to die back, cut off the seedhead and hang it upside-down to ripen. Reserve some seeds for next year and then hang the seedhead outside for the birds.

PLANT SEEDS IN SPRING AND SEEDLINGS IN SUMMER TO FLOWER IN LATE SUMMER

1 Line the base of the pot with drainage material and fill with the compost (soil mix). Scoop out evenly spaced holes for each seedling and plant, firming the compost around the plants.

2 Scatter 1 tablespoon of plant food granules on the surface of the compost (soil mix). Place in a sunny position, out of the wind, and water regularly.

Alpine sink

An old stone sink is a perfect container for a collection of alpine plants. The rock helps to create the effect of a miniature landscape and provides shelter for some of the plants. The sink is set up on the stand of an old sewing machine so that the plants can be admired easily.

MATERIALS

Stone sink or trough 76 x 50cm (30 x 20in)
Crocks (broken pots) or other suitable drainage material
Moss-covered rock
Loam-based compost (soil mix) with 1/3 added coarse grit
Washed gravel

PLANTS

Achillea tomentosa
Veronica peduncularis
Hebe
Ivy
Sedum ewersii
Aster natalensis
Alpine willow (Salix alpina)
Arabis ferdinandi-coburgi 'Variegata'

HEBE

SEDUM

ACHILLEA

IVY

VERONICA

1 Cover the drainage hole of the sink with crocks (broken pots). Position the rock. Do this before adding the soil to create the effect of a natural rocky outcrop. Pour the compost (soil mix) into the sink.

2 Plan the position of your plants so that the end result will have a good balance of shape and colour. If the sink is very shallow you will need to scoop out the soil right to the base before planting but alpine plants are used to shallow soil. Make sure that the bottom leaves of low-growing plants are level with the soil. Too low and they will rot; too high and they will dry out.

3 When all the plants are in place, carefully pour washed gravel all around them to cover the whole soil area. Water and place in full or partial sun.

Late flowers

Although this windowbox is already looking good, towards the beginning of autumn it will really come into its own – by then the vibrant red and purple flowers of the pelargonium, salvias and lavenders will be at their most prolific.

MATERIALS

60cm (24in) wooden planter, stained black
Polystyrene (plastic foam) or other suitable drainage material
Compost (soil mix)
Slow-release plant food granules

PLANTS

Pelargonium 'Tomcat'
2 Lavenders (Lavandula pinnata)
2 Salvia 'Raspberry Royal'
2 blue brachycome daisies
Convolvulus sabatius
6 rose-pink alyssum

CONVOLVULUS   ALYSSUM

LAVENDER   BRACHYCOME

SALVIA

PELARGONIUM

1 Line the base of the container with polystyrene (plastic foam) or similar drainage material. Fill the windowbox with compost (soil mix), working in 3 teaspoons of slow-release plant food granules. Plant the pelargonium at the back of the windowbox, in the centre.

2 Plant the two lavenders in the rear corners of the box.

3 Plant the salvias at the front on either side of the pelargonium.

4 Plant the brachycome daisies in the front corners of the windowbox.

5 Plant the convolvulus in the centre, in front of the pelargonium.

6 Fill the spaces with the alyssum. Water well and place in a sunny position.

GARDENER'S TIP

Both the lavenders and the salvias are highly aromatic, so if possible position this box near a door or a path, so that you can enjoy the fragrance as you brush against the plants.

PLANT IN EARLY SUMMER

Autumn hanging basket

Towards the end of the season the colours of summer hanging baskets do not always marry happily with the reds and golds of autumn. This is the time to plant a richly coloured hanging basket for winter.

MATERIALS

30cm (12in) hanging basket
Plastic pot
Sphagnum moss
Equal mix loam-based compost (soil mix) and container compost
Slow-release plant food granules

PLANTS

4 winter-flowering pansies
3 variegated ivies
Euonymus fortunei ('Emerald and Gold' was used here)
2 dahlias

PANSY   DAHLIA   IVY   EUONYMUS

GARDENER'S TIP

Although special composts (soil mixes) with water-retaining gel are a boon for summer baskets, they can get water-logged in later months. Mix equal parts of loam-based and container composts for autumn and winter planting.

PLANT IN SPRING OR SUMMER TO FLOWER IN AUTUMN

1 Support the hanging basket on a pot. Unhook the chain from one fixing point so that it hangs down one side of the basket. Line the base and bottom half of basket with a generous layer of sphagnum moss.

2 Pour in compost (soil mix) until it is level with the top of the moss. Plant a layer of three pansies and three ivies, passing the foliage through the wire of the basket, so that the root-balls of the plants are resting on the compost.

3 Line the rest of the basket with moss and top up with compost (soil mix), firming it around the roots of the ivies and pansies. Then plant the remaining plants in the top of the basket, with the euonymus in the centre and the remaining pansy and dahlias surrounding it. Scatter a tablespoon of slow-release plant food granules on to the compost and water the hanging basket well. Re-attach the chain and hang the basket in full or partial sun.

Heather windowbox

This is a perfect project for an absolute beginner as it is extremely simple to achieve. The bark windowbox is a sympathetic container for the heathers, which look quite at home in their bed of moss.

MATERIALS

30cm (12in) bark windowbox
Crocks (broken pots) or other
* suitable drainage material*
Ericaceous compost (soil mix)
Bun moss

PLANTS

Heathers

HEATHERS

GARDENER'S TIP

Do not be tempted to use ordinary compost (soil mix) as it contains lime which, with few exceptions, is not suitable for the majority of heathers.

PLANT IN AUTUMN

1 Put a layer of crocks or other suitable drainage material in the bottom of the box.

2 Remove the heathers from their pots and position them in the windowbox.

3 Fill the gaps between the plants with the compost (soil mix), pressing it around the plants. Water in well.

4 Tuck the bun moss snugly around the plants so that no soil is visible. Place in full or partial sun.

Evergreens with extra colour

They may be easy to look after but all-year-round window-boxes can start to look a bit lifeless after a couple of seasons. It does not take much trouble to add a few seasonal flowers and it makes all the difference to a display.

MATERIALS

76cm (30in) plastic windowbox
Compost (soil mix)
Slow-release plant food granules

PLANTS

Hebe *'Baby Marie'*
Convolvulus cneorum
Potentilla *'Nunk'*
Variegated ivies
2 Diascia *'Ruby Field'*
Pink marguerite (Argyranthemum *'Flamingo'*)

IVY

CONVOLVULUS

POTENTILLA

MARGUERITE

DIASCIA

HEBE

1 Check the drainage holes are open in the base and, if not, drill or punch them open. Fill the windowbox with compost (soil mix), adding in 3 teaspoons of slow-release plant food granules. Plant the hebe in the centre.

2 Plant the convolvulus near one end of the windowbox.

3 Plant the potentilla near the other end of the windowbox.

4 Plant the two ivies at the front corners of the windowbox.

5 Plant the diascias on either side of the hebe at the front of the windowbox.

6 Plant the marguerite between the hebe and the convolvulus at the back. Water well and stand in full or partial sun.

GARDENER'S TIP

When the diascias and marguerite finish flowering, take them out, feed the remaining plants with more granules, and fill the spaces with winter-flowering plants such as pansies or heathers.

PLANT IN SPRING

Japanese-style planter

Fully hardy, the deciduous Japanese maple turns a brilliant orange, red or yellow in autumn. The tree is surrounded by moss and stones to create the effect of a Japanese garden. This planted container is designed to be very lightweight and would be ideal for a roof terrace or balcony.

MATERIALS

Apple barrel or similar wooden tub
Plastic saucer to fit the bottom of the container
Slow-release plant food granules
Polystyrene (plastic foam) packing material
Bun moss
Large stones

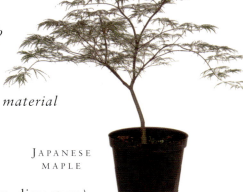

JAPANESE
MAPLE

PLANT

Japanese maple (Acer palmatum var. dissectum)

GARDENER'S TIP

The tree should be checked annually to see if it needs repotting. If roots are showing through the base of the pot this is a sure sign that the tree should be moved into a larger one. If weight is not a consideration use clay granules instead of polystyrene (plastic foam).

PLANT AT ANY TIME OF THE YEAR

1 Place the plastic saucer in the base of the container.

2 Stand the tree in its pot in the saucer. Scatter half a table-spoon of plant food granules on the surface of the compost (soil mix). Fill the area around the pot with polystyrene (plastic foam).

3 Cover the surface of the perlite or polystyrene with bun moss interspersed with stones. Place in full or partial sun and water regularly.

Foliage wall pot

The bushy growth of *Fuchsia magellanica* 'Alba Variegata' is ideal for displaying as a crown of leafy hair in a head-shaped wall pot. This copy of an ancient Grecian head will add a classical touch to a modern garden.

MATERIALS

Grecian head wall pot
Expanded clay granules

PLANTS

Fuchsia magellanica *'Alba Variegata'*

FUCHSIA

1 Check that the wall pot has a hook or can be hung up. The hanging point will need to be sufficiently strong to carry the weight of a moist pot.

2 Add expanded clay granules to the base of the wall pot to lift the top of the plant to the right level.

3 Place the plant in its pot inside the wall pot.

4 Arrange the foliage to make a convincing leafy crown of hair for the head.

GARDENER'S TIP

Check the base of the pot for drainage holes. If there are no holes, you will need to remove the pot each time you water it, allowing the compost to drain before replacing it.

PLANT AT ANY TIME OF YEAR

Winter Containers

Winter-flowering pansies, planted in a trug or old basket, will bloom throughout the season and can be moved to provide colour whererever it is needed. Evergreen plants come in different shapes, sizes and colours and provide year-round interest. Box trees planted in simple terracotta pots draw the eye and an evergreen standard holly tree, surrounded by pine cones, is decorative for Christmas.

Be bold and try short-term plants too. Cape heathers and winter cherries will look good for a few weeks even in cold and frosty weather.

Classic topiary

MATERIALS

4 large terracotta pots
Bark chippings
Crocks (broken pots) or other
  suitable drainage material
Equal mix loam-based compost
  (soil mix) and container compost
Slow-release plant food granules

PLANTS

4 box trees (Buxus sempervirens)
in different topiary shapes

BOX TREES (*BUXUS SEMPERVIRENS*)

The clean lines of the topiary are matched by the simplicity of the terracotta pots. Since the eye is drawn to the outlines of the box plants, decorated pots would be a distraction.

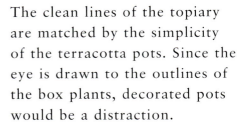

1 If the plant has been well looked after in the nursery it may not need potting on yet. In this case simply slip the plant in its pot into the terracotta container.

2 To conserve moisture and conceal the plastic pot, cover with a generous layer of bark chippings.

3 To repot a box tree, first place a good layer of crocks or other drainage material in the bottom of the pot. Remove the tree from its plastic pot and place it in the terracotta container. Surround the root-ball with compost (soil mix), pushing it well down the sides.

4 Scatter a tablespoon of plant food granules on top of the compost (soil mix) and top with a layer of bark chippings. Water well and position in sun or partial shade.

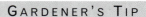
GARDENER'S TIP

Don't get carried away when you trim topiary. Little and often, with an ordinary pair of scissors, is better than occasional dramatic gestures with a pair of shears.

PLANT AT ANY
TIME OF THE YEAR

Trug of winter pansies

Winter pansies are wonderfully resilient and will bloom bravely throughout the winter as long as they are regularly dead-headed. This trug may be moved around to provide colour wherever it is needed, and acts as a perfect antidote to mid-winter gloom.

MATERIALS

Old wooden trug
Sphagnum moss
Compost (soil mix)
Slow-release plant food granules

PLANTS

15 winter-flowering pansies (violas)

PANSIES

1 Line the trug with a layer of sphagnum moss. Fill the moss lining with compost (soil mix).

2 Plant the pansies by starting at one end and filling the spaces between the plants with compost (soil mix) as you go. Gently firm each plant into position and add a final layer of compost mixed with a tablespoon of plant food granules around the pansies. Water and place in a fairly sunny position.

GARDENER'S TIP

Not everyone has an old trug available, but an old basket, colander, or an enamel bread bin could be used instead. Junk shops and flea markets are a great source of containers that are too battered for their original use, but fine for planting.

PLANT IN AUTUMN TO FLOWER IN WINTER

Evergreen garden

Evergreen plants come in many shapes, sizes and shades. Grouped in containers they will provide you with year-round interest and colour.

MATERIALS

Terracotta pots of various sizes
Crocks (broken pots) or similar drainage material
Equal mix loam-based compost (soil mix) and container compost
Plant saucers
Gravel
Slow-release plant food granules

PLANTS

False cypress (Chamaecyparis lawsoniana 'Columnaris'; C. pisifera 'Filifera Aurea')
Berberis darwinii
Berberis thunbergii 'Atropurpurea Nana'
Pachysandra terminalis
Bergenia

FALSE CYPRESS

BERGENIA

BERBERIS

PACHYSANDRA

GARDENER'S TIP

Include some golden or variegated foliage amongst your evergreens and choose contrasting leaf forms to make a striking group.

PLANT AT ANY
TIME OF THE YEAR

1 Large shrubs, such as this conifer, should be potted into a proportionally large container. Place plenty of crocks (broken pots) at the base of the pot. If the plant is at all potbound, tease the roots loose before planting in its new pot. Fill around the root-ball with compost (soil mix), pressing it down firmly around the edges of the pot.

2 Smaller plants, like bergenia, should be planted in a larger pot than the original. Place crocks in the base of the pot, position the plant and then fill around the edges with compost (soil mix). Repeat with the remaining plants.

3 Plants will stay moist longer if they are stood in saucers of wet gravel. This group of plants will do well positioned in partial shade. Water regularly and feed with slow-release plant food granules in the spring and autumn.

Year-round windowbox

In the same way that a garden has certain plants that provide structure throughout the year, this window box has been planted so that there is always plenty of foliage. Extra colour may be introduced each season by including small flowering plants, such as heathers.

MATERIALS

90cm (3ft) wooden windowbox, preferably self-watering
Equal mix loam-based compost (soil mix) and container compost
Slow-release plant food granules
Bark chippings

PLANTS

Skimmia reevesiana *'Rubella'*
2 Arundinaria pygmaea
2 Cotoneaster conspicuus
2 *periwinkles* (Vinca minor *'Variegata'*)
6 *heathers*

PERIWINKLE   COTONEASTER   SKIMMIA   ARUNDINARIA   HEATHER

1 If you are using a self-watering container, feed the wicks through the base of the plastic liner. Slip the liner into the wooden windowbox.

2 Before you start planting, plan the position of the plants so that the colours and shapes look well balanced. Remove the plants from their pots, tease loose their roots if they look at all potbound and position in the windowbox. Top up with compost (soil mix).

3 Once the structure plants are in place you can add the colour; in this case, the heathers. Scoop out a hole for each heather and then plant, pressing firmly around each one. Scatter two tablespoons of plant food granules over the surface.

4 Top-dress the windowbox with a layer of bark chippings; this will help to conserve moisture. Water thoroughly.

GARDENER'S TIP

Plants do not need watering in winter, unless they are sheltered from the rain. Even then they should be watered sparingly and not in frosty weather. Self-watering containers should be drained before winter to prevent frost damage.

PLANT AT ANY
TIME OF THE YEAR

Gothic ivy

Twisted willow branches set into a chimney pot offer an attractive support for ivy, and will provide welcome interest in the winter.

MATERIALS

Chimney pot
Compost (soil mix)
90cm (3ft) wire netting

PLANTS

4–5 branches of twisted willow
Large ivy (Hedera helix var. hibernica was used here)

IVY

1 Place the chimney pot in its final position (in shade or half-shade) and half-fill with compost (soil mix). Fold or crumple the wire netting down into the chimney pot so that it rests on the compost.

2 Arrange the willow branches in the chimney pot, pushing the stems through the wire netting.

3 Rest the ivy, in its pot, on the wire netting amongst the willow branches. Fill the chimney pot with compost (soil mix) to within 10cm (4in) of the rim. Cut loose any ties and remove the cane.

4 Arrange the stems of ivy over the willow branches and water. To start with it may look rather contrived, but as the ivy settles into its new surroundings it will attach itself to the willow.

GARDENER'S TIP

You may find that some of your twisted willow branches take root in the compost (soil mix). Plant a rooted branch in the garden where it will grow into a tree. It will eventually be quite large so do not plant it near the house.

PLANT AT ANY TIME OF THE YEAR

An evergreen wall basket

Pansies will flower throughout the winter. Even if they are flattened by rain, frost or snow, at the first sign of improvement in the weather their heads will pop up again to bring brightness to the dullest day. They have been planted with ivies to provide colour from early autumn through to late spring.

MATERIALS

30cm (12in) wall basket
Sphagnum moss
Compost (soil mix)

PLANTS

2 golden variegated ivies
2 copper pansies (viola)
Yellow pansy (viola)

PANSIES

IVY

GARDENER'S TIP

Winter baskets do not need regular feeding and should only be watered in very dry conditions. To prolong the flowering life of the pansies, dead-head regularly and pinch out any straggly stems to encourage new shoots from the base.

PLANT IN AUTUMN

1 Line the basket with moss. Three-quarters fill the basket with compost (soil mix) and position the ivies with their root-balls resting on the compost. Guide the stems through the sides of the basket so that they trail downwards. Pack more moss around the ivies and top up the basket with compost.

2 Plant the two copper pansies at either end of the basket.

3 Plant the yellow pansy in the centre. Water well and hang in shade or semi-shade.

Winter cheer

Many windowboxes are left unplanted through the winter, but you can soon brighten the house or garden during this season with an easy arrangement of pot-grown plants plunged in bark.

MATERIALS

40cm (16in) glazed windowbox
Bark chippings

PLANTS

2 miniature conifers
2 variegated ivies
2 red polyanthus

POLYANTHUS   CONIFER

IVY

1 Water all the plants. Place the conifers, still in their pots, at each end of the windowbox.

2 Half-fill the windowbox with bark chippings.

3 Place the pots of polyanthus on the bark chippings between the two conifers.

4 Place the pots of ivy in the front corners of the windowbox. Add further bark chippings to the container until all the pots are concealed. Water only when plants show signs of dryness. Stand in any position.

GARDENER'S TIP

When it is time to replant the windowbox, plunge the conifers, still in their pots, in a shady position in the garden. Water well through the spring and summer and they may be used again next year.

PLANT IN EARLY WINTER

Classic winter colours

Convolvulus cneorum is an attractive small shrub with eye-catching silver-grey leaves, which last through winter, and white flowers in spring and summer. Planted with ice-blue pansies, it makes a softly subtle display from autumn to spring.

MATERIALS

30cm (12in) hanging basket
Sphagnum moss
Compost (soil mix)

PLANTS

*8 silver/blue pansies (Viola
    'Silver Wings', or similar)*
Convolvulus cneorum

CONVOLVULUS

PANSIES

1 Half-line the basket with moss and fill with compost (soil mix) to the top of the moss. Plant four of the pansies into the side of the basket by placing their root-balls on the compost, and gently guiding the leaves through the side of the basket.

2 Line the rest of the basket with moss and top up with compost (soil mix). Plant the convolvulus in the basket centre.

3 Plant the remaining four pansies around the convolvulus. Water well and hang in sun or partial shade.

GARDENER'S TIP

At the end of the winter cut back any dead wood or straggly branches on the *Convolvulus cneorum*, and give a liquid feed to encourage new growth. Small shrubs such as this may be used in hanging baskets for one season, but will then need planting into a larger container or the border.

PLANT IN AUTUMN

Golden Christmas holly

Evergreen standard holly trees are splendid container plants. This golden holly in a gilded pot has been dressed up for Christmas with bows and baubles.

HOLLY

MATERIALS

40cm (16in) terracotta pot
Gold spray-paint
Crocks (broken pots) or
    similar drainage material
Composted manure
Loam-based compost (soil mix)
Pine cones
90cm (3ft) wired ribbon
Tin Christmas decorations

PLANTS

Golden holly

1 Spray the pot with gold paint and leave to dry. Place a good layer of drainage material in the base. Cover with a 7.5cm (3in) layer of composted manure and a thin layer of loam-based potting compost (soil mix). Remove the holly from its existing container and place in the gilded pot.

2 Surround the root-ball with compost (soil mix), pressing down firmly to ensure that the tree is firmly planted, and cover the surface with pine cones.

3 Tie the ribbon into a bow around the trunk of the tree. Spray the decorations gold and hang in the branches. Water the tree to settle it in, but do not do this on a frosty day.

GARDENER'S TIP

In the autumn, plant some corms of *Iris reticulata* or similar small bulbs in the compost (soil mix) surrounding the tree for a delightful spring display.

PLANT IN AUTUMN, WINTER OR SPRING

Index